SEEDS OF LOVE

A COUPLE'S JOURNAL

—

KEMI AND BODE OLUTUNBI

SYNCTERFACE™
Syncterface Media
London
www.syncterfacemedia.com

THIS
JOURNAL
IS PRESENTED

To

_____

From

_____

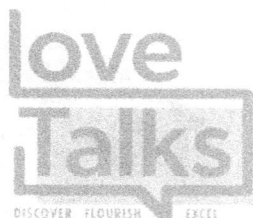

The Five Love languages © Gary Chapman © 1992

SEEDS OF LOVE
(A COUPLE'S JOURNAL)
52 WEEKLY DEVOTIONS TO GROW CLOSER TO GOD AND EACH OTHER
ISBN: 978-1-912896-25-7
Copyright © 2022 Kemi and Bode Olutunbi

Cover design by Dami Odukoya Design

Published in the United Kingdom by Syncterface Media, London

This book is printed on acid-free paper

Foreword

Keeping God at the heart of your marriage is the key to having a successful and happy marriage. The word of God offers so much wisdom on how to build strong and healthy marriages. This devotional, Seeds of Love, draws on that wisdom, offering couples an opportunity to learn and grow in their love for God and for each other.

Filled with honest and heart-warming stories of Bode and Kemi's marriage journey, Godly principles and practical wisdom, it encourages the reader on their own journey. It is a useful resource for couples seeking to build strong and healthy marriages.

Look forward to a wonderful experience as you go through the pages.

~ Agu Irukwu ~

Senior Pastor
Jesus House for All the Nations

Welcome

We are passionate about marriage and this couple's journal was borne out of our desire to create an opportunity for couples to learn and grow in their love for God and each other.

Journaling together draws you closer as a couple and helps to bring your goals, hopes, and dreams alive. We hope that this will be a wonderful way for you to thank God for your marriage and share your appreciation for one another.

Our journaling journey has been a source of great encouragement to us as we have seen hopes, dreams, and ideas come to fruition. We are also aware of hopes, dreams, and prayers yet unfulfilled and journaling has helped us to keep our focus on God whilst trusting Him.

There are a variety of ways you can use this Journal. We have chosen a weekly format and each week has a topic, scripture, and reflection point. This gives you an opportunity to share and write your collective thoughts.

Before you start we would like you to take time out to discuss what you both hope to accomplish, including things that are most important to you both. This is your keepsake so we encourage you to personalise it by adding photos, cards, and any other items that you want to remember.

Our prayer for you is that as you read the scriptures together, the Holy Spirit will inspire your thoughts, the scriptures will come alive and God will share His heart, plans and purposes for you as a couple.

We would like to encourage you to use the companion Seeds of Love Couple's Devotional with this Journal.

Please also share your stories with us at
seedsoflove@lovetalks.tv

Join us at
www.lovetalks.tv

@LOVETALKSTV

May God bless and preserve your marriage.

In His love and ours,
~ Kemi and Bode Olutunbi ~

Contents

LOYALTY FORGIVE PASSION OPENESS
CONNECT
FUN
FORGIVE INSPIRE
OPENESS LOYALTY OPENESS
CONNECTO
KINDNESS
PASSION O FUN
JOY LOVE
FORGIVE LOYALTY

God's Design for Marriage

Genesis 2:18-25

....

....

....

....

....

....

....

....

....

....

....

....

....

....

....

....

....

....

....

....

....

Heart2Heart
In what ways do you need to accept your spouse as a gift to you?

Marriage - A Safe Haven

Isaiah 32:2

....

....

....

....

....

....

....

....

....

....

....

....

....

....

....

....

....

....

....

....

Heart2Heart
What do you need from your spouse to experience a safe haven marriage?

A Vision for Your Marriage

Habakkuk 2:2-3

Heart2Heart
How are you working as a team to fulfil God's vision for your marriage?

Sex - A Divine Gift

(PART 1)

Song of Solomon 7:1-9

Heart2Heart

How can you make your sex life more fulfilling?

Sex - A Divine Gift

(PART 2)

1 Corinthians 7:2-5

....

....

....

....

....

....

....

....

....

....

....

....

....

....

....

....

....

....

....

....

Heart2Heart

What is your attitude towards sex. Is there anything holding you back from fully enjoying sex?

The Gift of Oneness

Genesis 2:24-25

....

....

....

....

....

....

....

....

....

....

....

....

....

....

....

....

....

....

....

Heart2Heart
Are there ways in which you are drifting away from each other and
not embracing the gift of oneness in your marriage? How can you
stop this drift?

Loving Your Wife

1Peter 3:7

···

···

···

···

···

···

···

···

···

···

···

···

···

···

···

···

···

···

Heart2Heart

Ask your wife what loving her means to her. In what ways can you show love to her this week?

Honouring Your Husband

1 Peter 3:1-2

....
....
....
....
....
....
....
....
....
....
....
....
....
....
....
....
....

....

....

....

....

....

....

....

....

....

....

....

....

....

....

....

....

....

....

....

Heart2Heart
Ask your husband what honouring him means to him. In what ways can you honour him this week?

A Mutual Responsibility to Love

Ephesians 5:21,25-29

....

....

....

....

....

....

....

....

....

....

....

....

....

....

....

....

....

....

....

....

Heart2Heart
(Husband) In what ways can you show sacrificial leadership?
(Wife) In what ways can you show submission?.

God's Plans For Your Marriage

Jeremiah 29:11

....

....

....

....

....

....

....

....

....

....

....

....

....

....

....

....

....

....

....

....

Heart2Heart
What do you know about God's plan for your marriage?

Pillars of a Successful Marriage

CLEAVING

Genesis 2:24

....

....

....

....

....

....

....

....

....

....

....

....

....

....

....

....

....

....

....

....

Heart2Heart

What can you do to cleave more closely to each other?

Pillars of a Successful Marriage

ONENESS

Genesis 2:24

....

....

....

....

....

....

....

....

....

....

....

....

....

....

....

....

....

....

....

....

Heart2Heart
In what ways can you actively pursue oneness in your marriage?

Pillars of a Successful Marriage

NAKED AND UNASHAMED
Genesis 2:24

Heart2Heart
What steps can you take to be more vulnerable with each other?

Pillars of a Successful Marriage

INTIMACY (PART 1)

Genesis 2:25

....

....

....

....

....

....

....

....

....

....

....

....

....

....

....

....

....

....

Heart2Heart
What can you do to communicate better with each other?

Pillars of a Successful Marriage

INTIMACY (PART 2)

Genesis 2:25

....

....

....

....

....

....

....

....

....

....

....

....

....

....

....

....

....

....

....

....

....

....

Heart2Heart

In what ways can you increase emotional, physical and spiritual intimacy in your marriage?

Pillars of a Successful Marriage

INTIMACY (PART 3)

Genesis 2:25

....

....

....

....

....

....

....

....

....

....

....

....

....

....

....

....

....

....

....

Heart2Heart

What steps do you need to take to foster a safe environment for open and honest communication in your relationship?

Pillars of a Successful Marriage

LISTENING: THE WAY TO YOUR WIFE'S HEART

James 1:19

....

....

....

....

....

....

....

....

....

....

....

....

....

....

....

....

....

....

....

....

Heart2Heart
Ask your wife to share the things you can do to make her feel listened to.

Pillars of a Successful Marriage

RESPECT: THE WAY TO YOUR HUSBAND'S HEART

1 Peter 3:2

Heart2Heart
Are your words or tone of voice showing respect to your husband?

Loving Against All Odds

Philippians 2:4

....

....

....

....

....

....

....

....

....

....

....

....

....

....

....

....

....

....

....

Heart2Heart
In what ways can you build your (phileo) friendship in your marriage?

Your Number One Priority

John 15:13

....
....
....
....
....
....
....
....
....
....
....
....
....
....
....
....
....
....
....
....
....

Heart2Heart
How can you demonstrate that you are each other's priority this
week?

Protecting Your Marriage

AFFAIR PROOF YOUR MARRIAGE

Ecclesiastes 10:8

....

....

....

....

....

....

....

....

....

....

....

....

....

....

....

....

....

....

....

....

Heart2Heart
In what ways can you affair-proof your marriage?

Protecting Your Marriage

LET GO OF PAST RELATIONSHIPS

Song of Solomon 2:15

....

....

....

....

....

....

....

....

....

....

....

....

....

....

....

....

....

....

....

....

Heart2Heart
What past and/or harmful relationships do you need to let go of?

Protecting Your Marriage

LAY ASIDE THE WEIGHT

Hebrews 12:1

···

···

···

···

···

···

···

···

···

···

···

···

···

···

···

···

···

···

···

···

Heart2Heart
Are there any past experiences hindering your marriage relationship?

Protecting Your Marriage

GUARD YOUR HEART

Proverbs 4:23

....

....

....

....

....

....

....

....

....

....

....

....

....

....

....

....

....

....

....

....

Heart2Heart

In what way do you need to guard your heart and protect your marriage?

Choose Life

Romans 6:23

....

....

....

....

....

....

....

....

....

....

....

....

....

....

....

....

....

....

....

....

....

....

Heart2Heart
What temptations do you need to overcome in your marriage?

Marriage Robber

STRIFE
John 10:10

_____

_____

_____

_____

_____

_____

_____

_____

_____

_____

_____

_____

_____

_____

_____

_____

....

....

....

....

....

....

....

....

....

....

....

....

....

....

....

....

....

....

....

Heart2Heart
How do you resolve conflict? Is it healthy?

Marriage Robber

SELFISHNESS

Philippians 2:3-4

....

....

....

....

....

....

....

....

....

....

....

....

....

....

....

....

....

....

....

....

....

....

Heart2Heart

In what ways have you been selfish in your marriage? What can you do to make amends?

Marriage Robber

THE ENEMY WITHIN - NEGATIVE THOUGHTS

Philippians 4:8

....

....

....

....

....

....

....

....

....

....

....

....

....

....

....

....

....

....

....

....

....

....

....

....

....

....

....

....

....

....

....

....

....

....

....

....

....

Heart2Heart
What negative thoughts about your spouse and marriage do you
need to let go of?

The Blame Game

Matthew 7:5

....

....

....

....

....

....

....

....

....

....

....

....

....

....

....

....

....

....

....

....

Heart2Heart

In what ways do I play the blame game in our marriage? (Reflect on your own and discuss)

Make Every Day Count

Ephesians 5:15-16

....

....

....

....

....

....

....

....

....

....

....

....

....

....

....

....

....

....

....

....

Heart2Heart

In what way is the enemy stealing your time with each other? What can you do to avoid the little things that become bones of contention?

Investments in Your Marriage

A THREE-FOLD CORD

Ecclesiastes 4:9-12

....

....

....

....

....

....

....

....

....

....

....

....

....

....

....

....

....

....

Heart2Heart
In what ways can you better support each other?

Investments in Your Marriage
PRAYER: THE BEST GIFT YOU CAN GIVE
Ecclesiastes 4:9-12

Heart2Heart
Share your prayer needs with each other. Both the small and big
things. Pray for each other.

Investments in Your Marriage

PRAYING TOGETHER

Ecclesiastes 4:9-12

....

....

....

....

....

....

....

....

....

....

....

....

....

....

....

....

....

....

....

Heart2Heart
In what ways can you improve your prayer times together?

Keeping The Flames of Love Alive

Song of Solomon 8:6-7

Heart2Heart

What can you do to keep igniting passion and romance in your marriage?

Deposits in Your Love Bank

PART 1

Galatians 6:9

Heart2Heart
In what ways can you put love deposits into your marriage?

Deposits in Your Love Bank

PART 2

Proverbs 19:11

....

....

....

....

....

....

....

....

....

....

....

....

....

....

....

....

....

....

....

....

....

Heart2Heart

Are you holding any hurt against your spouse? Is there anything you need to share with each other?

Deposits in Your Love Bank

PART 3
Proverbs 17:9

....
....
....
....
....
....
....
....
....
....
....
....
....
....
....
....
....
....
....
....
....
....

Heart2Heart
Identify and discuss any issue you need to ask or offer forgiveness for.

Deposits in Your Love Bank

PART 4

1 Corinthians 13:4

....

....

....

....

....

....

....

....

....

....

....

....

....

....

....

....

....

....

....

....

Heart2Heart
In what ways do you need to be more patient with your spouse?

Enjoying Your Wife

Proverbs 5:18

Heart2Heart
In what ways can you celebrate your love for each other?

Speaking The Truth in Love

Ephesians 4:15, 29

Heart2Heart

In what ways do you need to change your communication style to reflect truth and grace?

Responding to Change

PART 1

Ecclesiastes 3:1-8

....

....

....

....

....

....

....

....

....

....

....

....

....

....

....

....

....

....

Heart2Heart

How are you responding to changes in your marriage journey?
What changes do you need to accept in each other?

Responding to Change

PART 2

Romans 12:1-2

....

....

....

....

....

....

....

....

....

....

....

....

....

....

....

....

....

....

....

Heart2Heart

What mindset do you have about your marriage that needs to change?

Blended Gifts

Genesis 5:2 (NIV)

....

....

....

....

....

....

....

....

....

....

....

....

....

....

....

....

....

....

....

....

....

....

....

....

....

....

....

....

....

....

....

....

....

....

....

....

....

....

....

Heart2Heart
List five differences between you and your spouse. How can these differences make your marriage more balanced and complete?

Money Talks

Luke 14:28-29

Heart2Heart
How are you building financial intimacy in your marriage?

Knowing You, Knowing Me

Colossians 3:12

....

....

....

....

....

....

....

....

....

....

....

....

....

....

....

....

....

....

....

....

....

....

....

....

....

....

....

....

....

....

....

....

....

Heart2Heart
What does your spouse need from you at this time? Ask each other.

Expressions of Love

PART 1

Song of Solomon 8:7

....

....

....

....

....

....

....

....

....

....

....

....

....

....

....

....

....

....

....

....

Heart2Heart
In what ways can you show commitment to your spouse?

Expressions of Love

PART 2

Song of Solomon 8:7

....

....

....

....

....

....

....

....

....

....

....

....

....

....

....

....

....

....

....

....

....

....

....

....

....

....

....

....

....

....

....

....

....

....

....

....

....

Heart2Heart

Discuss your love language with each other. How can you make your spouse feel deeply loved this week?

A Godly Heritage

Proverbs 14:26

....

....

....

....

....

....

....

....

....

....

....

....

....

....

....

....

....

....

....

....

....

Heart2Heart
How can you help your children build their relationship with God?

Your Legacy

Ephesians 6:4

....

....

....

....

....

....

....

....

....

....

....

....

....

....

....

....

....

....

....

....

....

....

....

....

....

....

....

....

....

....

....

....

....

....

....

....

....

....

....

....

Heart2Heart
How would your children describe your marriage?

Praying For Your Child

James 5:16b

Heart2Heart
How can you pray for and with your child(ren)?

Lean on Me

Proverbs 13:20

··

··

··

··

··

··

··

··

··

··

··

··

··

··

··

··

Heart2Heart
Who are those couples around you whose influence strengthen
your marriage?

Treasures in Heavenly Places

Matthew 6:19-21

....

....

....

....

....

....

....

....

....

....

....

....

....

....

....

....

....

....

....

Heart2Heart
How can your marriage be a godly influence to those around you?

LOYALTY FORGIVE

CONNECT

FUN

FORGIVE

OPENESS LOYALTY

CONNECT

KINDNES

FUN

JOY

LOVE

FORGIVE LOYALTY

CONNECT

WITH US

AT

www.lovetalks.tv

@LOVETALKSTV

Kemi and Bode are a husband and wife team who do life together at home and at work. They are the co-founders of "Lovetalks", a mission-driven kingdom expression focusing on purpose, marriage, and healthy relationships. They also lead the marriage ministry in their local church. They are passionate about supporting others in pursuing and discovering their purpose in God, building strong marriages and fostering healthy relationships. They believe marriage is the foundation of family life, and family is at the core of a thriving society.

They were involved in the Marriage Course run by Holy Trinity Anglican Church in Brompton, London (HTB) and are both members of the steering committee for Engage, a national network of Christian organisations that focuses on different areas of a relationship. They are also one of the presenters featured in "Marriage By Design", a pre-marriage DVD series developed by Care for the Family, and have encouraged, taught, counselled, and coached countless couples in building healthy marriages and homes.

Kemi and Bode speak on purpose, marriage and healthy relationships at conferences and seminars, sharing Godly insights and practical nuggets. They are also trained facilitators, behavioural consultants, and marriage counsellors.